# Straight to the Source

# Magazines

John Hamilton

## ABDO
### Publishing Company

**visit us at**
**www.abdopub.com**

Published by ABDO Publishing Company, 4940 Viking Drive, Edina, Minnesota 55435.
Copyright © 2005 by Abdo Consulting Group, Inc. International copyrights reserved in all
countries. No part of this book may be reproduced in any form without written permission from
the publisher. The Checkerboard Library™ is a trademark and logo of ABDO Publishing
Company.

Printed in the United States.

Cover Photo: Corbis
Interior Photos: Corbis pp. 1, 5, 7, 9, 10, 11, 12, 13, 14, 15, 19, 20, 21, 23, 25, 27, 29;
    Getty Images pp. 12, 13, 17

Series Coordinator: Stephanie Hedlund
Editors: Kate A. Conley, Jennifer R. Krueger
Art Direction: Neil Klinepier

**Library of Congress Cataloging-in-Publication Data**

Hamilton, John, 1959-
    Magazines / John Hamilton.
        p. cm. -- (Straight to the source)
    Includes index.
    Summary: A look at the history and types of magazines, some famous magazines, parts of a
typical magazine, how they are made, and how they can be used to research a report.
    ISBN 1-59197-546-8
    1. Periodicals--Juvenile literature. [1. Periodicals.] I. Title.

PN4832.H36 2004
050--dc22
                                                                        2003062871

# Contents

# Magazines

Magazines have informed and entertained people for hundreds of years. The word *magazine* comes from an Arabic term that means "storehouse." Yet, it's hard to say exactly what a magazine is.

Basically, a magazine is a collection of articles that is published in regular time periods. This is why they are also called **periodicals**. Magazines are usually published every week or every month. Sometimes, there are even longer periods between printings.

There is a magazine for just about any subject you can imagine. No one knows for sure the number of periodicals published each year. Some people estimate there are 22,000 magazines in the United States alone. Others claim that there are more than 65,000.

Whatever the number, the influence of magazines is strong. People depend on them for information, entertainment, and current events. Some say magazines are nearly as important as television in reaching a large number of people!

*Magazines help people learn about their world.*

# Early Magazines

Some scholars believe publications resembling magazines started in ancient China. But, magazines as we know them began in Europe in the 1600s.

Many people at that time were just beginning to read. In fact, printing was a new industry. Magazines appeared after books and newspapers were established.

In the 1650s, book catalogs were commonly inserted into newspapers. These catalogs were later accompanied by book reviews. Soon, the catalogs developed into separate publications called magazines.

Eventually, magazines began to cover other areas of interest. Journals and scholarly **periodicals** followed, as well as entertainment magazines.

One of the earliest magazines was *Erbauliche Monaths-Unterredungen*. It was published in Germany from 1663 to 1668. Another pioneering magazine, *Journal des Savants*, was published in Paris, France, in 1665.

**Opposite page:** *Johannes Gutenberg made printing easier when he invented a press around 1450. This press from the 1500s was an altered version of Gutenberg's design.*

As time passed, specialty publications grew and changed. Literary and scientific journals were regularly published. British magazines of the 1700s, such as the *Tatler* and the *Spectator*, were **forerunners** of today's **periodicals**.

In America, the first magazines were created in 1741 by two printers in Philadelphia, Pennsylvania. The first to appear was Andrew Bradford's *American Magazine*. Benjamin Franklin's *General Magazine* was published just three days after Bradford's magazine.

At that time, magazines had short **life spans**. For example, *American Magazine* lasted for only three monthly issues. Unlike books or newspapers, magazines were considered a luxury. And, most people didn't have enough money to buy magazines, or leisure time to read them.

**EXTRA!**

**Muckrakers**

Many magazines and newspapers focused on social reforms. Journalists who exposed bad working conditions or corrupt businesses and politicians were called muckrakers.

In 1825, fewer than 100 magazines existed. However, the industry boomed in the 1830s. By 1850, about 600 periodicals were being published. After that, the industry continued to grow.

*In the 1900s, magazines in the United States covered news, literature, and many other subjects.*

# Over Time

During the late 1800s and early 1900s, many magazines highlighted social reforms. One such magazine was the *Nation*. It was founded in 1865 as a weekly newspaper but later became a magazine.

Soon **periodicals**, such as *Harper's Magazine,* began publishing the works of famous American writers. *Harper's* published pieces by Mark Twain, Henry James, and Jack London.

Magazines with literary content led to general-interest magazines. These magazines became popular in the 1920s and 1930s. One example of a general-interest magazine is the *Saturday Evening Post*. It ran a large variety of stories that contained photographs.

In the 1920s, newsmagazines developed. Henry Luce and Briton Hadden were upset with the miseducation of people. They began *Time* magazine in

*By 1922, the* **Saturday Evening Post** *had a circulation of more than 2 million copies.*

STREET IN OLYMPIA, WASHINGTON TERRITORY.

North Pacific Railway. It is separated from the main land—but only by the Swinomish Slough, a broad marshy tract, which settlers are now dyking and draining, and turning into a point on the Columbia River, where it will connect with the line of river and railway communication already established by the Oregon Steamship Company. But this can be only a

1923. It informed and influenced millions of people, and it is still published today.

By the mid-1900s, magazines were popular across the country. However television use grew in the 1950s, leaving less advertising available for **periodicals**. For a while, this hurt the magazine industry. But it endured. Today, magazines provide reading material on nearly every topic.

# Famous People

*Sir Arthur Conan Doyle*

The **Strand** was a monthly magazine that was published from 1891 to 1950. It was one of the first periodicals to publish literature with illustrations. Produced in England, the Strand is most famous for printing Sir Arthur Conan Doyle's **Adventures of Sherlock Holmes**.

Harold Ross started the **New Yorker** magazine in 1925. He remained with the weekly magazine until he died in 1951. The **New Yorker** became famous for its literary articles, commentary, and humor. Today, it is still influential.

*Harold Ross*

## Briton Hadden

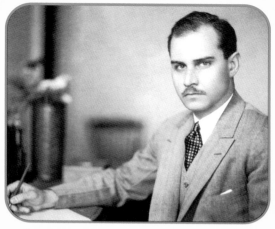

Henry Luce and Briton Hadden started a weekly newsmagazine called Time. They wanted Time to help people understand current events. The first issue of the magazine appeared in March 1923.

Hadden passed away in 1929. Luce went on to have a very successful publishing career. His company published other popular magazines such as Sports Illustrated, Life, and Fortune.

Henry Luce

## Helen Gurley Brown

Helen Gurley Brown became editor in chief of Cosmopolitan in 1959. She remade the magazine into an upbeat periodical for young women. It included advice on fashion, careers, and love. Cosmopolitan soon began outselling other women's magazines. Brown resigned in 1996.

# Today's Types

*Magazines that are printed on glossy paper are called glossies.*

There are many different magazines available today. Those you see at newsstands are only a fraction of the **periodicals** published. Many more are sent by mail and cover special interests.

General magazines are the kind of periodicals you see at the store. They are also called consumer magazines. They appeal to many people with broad interests.

General magazines include *Time*, *Newsweek*, and other newsmagazines. Women's magazines, such as *Redbook*, are also consumer **periodicals**. There are many other categories, including children's, outdoors, and business magazines.

Another type of periodical is the specialized, or trade, magazine. Trade magazines make up a huge, almost hidden industry. Nearly every profession or interest has its own special periodical. For example, *Publisher's Weekly* provides news for the publishing industry.

There are other categories of periodicals. These include literary journals and association magazines, such as *School Library Journal*. Digests are another type of periodical. *Reader's Digest* and others contain **condensed** versions of stories published elsewhere.

*People purchase magazines at newsstands or by subscription.*

# The Sections

All magazines have specialized features that attract readers. Something that is important in a consumer magazine may not be needed in a trade magazine. However, there are sections of magazines that are common to most **periodicals**.

Most magazines have a page or two devoted to an issue's table of contents (TOC). Many newsstand readers decide to buy an issue based mainly on its TOC. So, this section is designed to hook readers.

Many magazines set aside a page for the editor. This is called an editorial. In the past, a magazine editorial was the voice of the entire magazine. Often these editorials promoted social change.

Today, powerful editors who **crusade** for a cause are not common. So, magazine editorials do not take the **aggressive** stands they once did. Instead, a magazine's editorial usually recaps the current issue's content.

*Opposite page: A magazine's cover is also a way to catch a reader's attention.*

# O

## THE OPRAH
## MAGAZINE

# SUCCESS!
## Define it for yourself

## Never Say Never
Amazing women who
prove you can do anything

Fall's delicious
**new clothes**

What a charming guy!
**OPRAH talks to**
# TOM HANKS

OPRAH.COM
SEPTEMBER 2001 $3.50

Another common section called departments appears in each issue of a **periodical**. This section is usually found at the front of the magazine. Departments are shorter articles that are filled with news and current events.

These articles are most often written by a **freelance columnist** or the department's editor. Many magazine readers have a favorite department that they eagerly turn to. One example is the letters to the editor department, which lets readers express their views.

Feature articles are also common to most magazines. These stories are longer and contain more in-depth coverage than the articles in departments. These articles may be written by people who work on the magazine. More often, they are written by freelance writers.

Most features are 3,000 to 5,000 words long. Almost every feature is accompanied by some sort of illustration or photograph. Unlike books, many magazines rely heavily on **graphic** design to grab readers and keep their interest.

*You can be a freelance writer, too! There are many children's magazines that publish articles written by young writers.*

All of these magazine sections are planned well in advance. At any time, the staff is working on three issues of a magazine. They are working on the issue that is going to press and the one being written and designed. At the same time, they are planning the next issue.

# The Staff

Creating a magazine is a complicated process. Information must be collected and organized. Production must also be managed.  So, teams of people work together to create each issue.

Large general magazines sometimes employ a staff of hundreds.  Smaller magazines usually combine jobs so they can hire fewer people.  Some very small

*A publisher is often involved in planning each issue of a magazine.*

*Because of tight deadlines, the editor must work with other staff members to produce a magazine.*

**periodicals**, especially literary journals, might be run by only a handful of people.

One staff member every magazine has is the publisher. He or she handles the main business decisions and pays for creating the magazine. Today, large corporations or associations often act as publishers.

An editorial team is responsible for producing each issue's content. The person in charge is called the editor. On larger magazines, the editor is too busy to handle all the tasks that are necessary.

So, the editorial team includes other staff. The managing editor handles all the day-to-day details. Assistant editors work with **freelancers** and often write articles. Copy editors and editorial assistants check for errors and help out with other story details.

The editorial team often uses freelance writers. Many of these writers sell articles to several different magazines. Often, freelancers are experts in the field they are writing about.

The editorial team also works with a magazine's art team. This group designs each page of a publication, most often on a computer. Art directors, illustrators, and photographers all work together. They make the magazine as attractive as possible.

Other staff work in advertising and **circulation**. They make sure money is collected from **subscribers** and companies that purchased ad space.

**EXTRA!**

### Magazine Advertisements

Magazine advertising is a huge business. Few magazines can survive on subscriptions alone. So, most magazines try to sell at least one page of advertising for each page of editorial content. Many magazines are very expensive to advertise in. But, companies are willing to pay because magazines are a good way to reach specific groups of people.

There are several other teams in most magazines. These include marketing, communications, production, and business operations staff. All are required in order to keep a magazine running smoothly.

*Members of the art team determine which images and graphics will make a story easier to understand.*

# Printing

A magazine is first put together by its staff. After an issue is written, laid out, and corrected, it is sent to a printing facility.

At the printer, a **periodical** first goes to the prepress team. There, computer files from the publisher are used to make **negatives**. The prepress team produces full-color **proofs**, which show exactly how the magazine will look once it is printed.

Then, **printing plates** are made from the negatives. These plates contain all of a page's information. Producing the plates is the last stage before the magazine is actually printed.

Most magazines today use a printing method called offset lithography. In this method, a printing plate is coated with ink. The plate is pressed against a rubber "blanket," which then makes contact with the paper.

After printing, the pages are folded, cut, and bound together. Finally, the magazines are delivered. Some are sent to newsstands. But, most are sent by mail to **subscribers** across the country.

*During offset printing, pages may be printed on individual sheets, which is called sheetfed. Or, they may be printed on a huge roll, or web, of paper.*

# Finding Sources

A magazine can be a good place to find information for your school research paper. Because magazines are published less often than newspapers, their information is more complete and **accurate**. Yet, they are published often enough that the information is mostly up-to-date.

The best place to find magazine articles is a library. Libraries have hundreds of magazines. They also have **archives** of **periodicals**. You can locate a magazine by searching the library's catalog. Librarians are also very knowledgeable about where to look.

A librarian uses several reference tools to find a magazine. Some common tools include *Readers' Guide to Periodical Literature* and *Ulrich's International Periodicals Directory*. These publications list thousands of magazines from around the world.

The library isn't the only place to find magazines. Today, many magazines have Web sites on the **Internet**. They often post old issues of their publications. This is

*Some magazine articles and library catalogs can be found on the Internet. So, people can do research from home.*

useful in searching for information. However, some magazine Web sites may charge a fee to search their site.

Once you find the magazine article you need, you have to **evaluate** it. Don't believe something just because it is in print. Books, Web sites, and magazines may be **inaccurate**. Try to find the same fact in more than one article, preferably in a different magazine.

# Citing Magazines

After finding reliable information, it is time to write your research paper. It is important to write your paper in your own words. If you use the exact words of other authors without giving them credit, you are plagiarizing. This is the same as stealing.

To avoid plagiarizing, take detailed notes when gathering your information. Then paraphrase by writing the information in your own words.

Even when paraphrasing, you must credit other people's work in your research paper. This is called citing sources. Citation shows your readers where they might look for more information on your topic.

There are several styles to use when citing sources. The most common is Modern Language Association (MLA) style. MLA has a handbook that provides citation methods for many publications, including magazines. Ask your librarian for help, too.

**Opposite page:** *Magazines and other sources can be found in a library's archives. If you need help finding sources, ask a librarian for assistance.*

Magazines are full of information. They can easily add to the volume of knowledge about any given subject. Magazines aren't as permanent as books or as disposable as newspapers. So, they are good for research papers and entertainment.

# Glossary

**accurate** - free of errors.  Something with errors is inaccurate.

**aggressive** - displays hostility.

**archives** - organized records.

**circulation** - the number of copies of a newspaper or magazine that are sold over a given period.

**columnist** - someone who regularly writes a newspaper or magazine article about a particular subject.

**condense** - to make shorter or less wordy.

**crusade** - to take part in a campaign to advance a cause, especially for reform.

**evaluate** - to determine the meaning or importance of something.

**forerunner** - someone or something that indicates what is to come.

**freelance** - a person who sells work to anyone who will buy it.

**graphic** - of or relating to visual arts such as painting and photography.

**Internet** - a way to let computers share information with other computer networks around the world.

**life span** - the length of time an organization, paper, or individual exists.

**negative** - a film that is the opposite of an original image.  So, an item's areas that were light will be dark, and those that were dark will be light.

**periodical** - an item that is published at a fixed period of time.

**printing plate** - a cast or mold of a page of type to be printed.

**proof** - a trial impression that is used to find errors before printing.

**subscriber** - a person who agrees to receive and pay for a publication.

**aggressive** - uh-GREH-sihv

**citation** - seye-TAY-shun

**crusade** - kroo-SAYD

**editorial** - eh-duh-TAWR-ee-uhl

**plagiarism** - PLAY-juh-rih-zuhm

To learn more about magazines, visit ABDO Publishing Company on the World Wide Web at **www.abdopub.com**. Web sites about magazines are featured on our Book Links page. These links are routinely monitored and updated to provide the most current information available.

# Index